Compiled by
Frater Lachesis Peyton
Tat Tvam Asi

SAKLAS
PUBLISHING

The Libri of the Zelator

ISBN: 979-8-9943016-8-5

ZELATOR LIBRI

Official

$2^{\circ}=9\square$

Syllabus

V

A∴A∴

A Note on this Series

The volume you hold is one of a series of companions to the work of
the A∴A∴, the spiritual order established by Aleister Crowley and
George Cecil Jones in 1907 and governed, in its inner life, by
principles far older than either man. Each book in the series gathers
into a single binding the official *libri*—the instructional texts—
assigned to a particular grade of the Order.

The Probationer volume collects the writings that orient the
newcomer and outline the first practices. The Neophyte volume
presents the curriculum for those who have entered the Outer
College in earnest. The Zelator volume carries the aspirant further,
into deeper work with breath, will, memory, and the central
scriptures of Thelema. Additional volumes, corresponding to higher
grades, may follow in time.

The contents of each volume were determined by cross-referencing
three primary sources. The first is Liber CLXXXV, *Liber Collegii
Sancti*, the Class D document that sets out the official tasks,
examinations, and oaths for every grade from Probationer to Adept.
This text specifies which *libri* the aspirant at each grade is required to
study, memorize, or master. The second is Liber CCVII, the *Syllabus
of the Official Instructions of the* A∴A∴, which catalogues the full corpus
of Order publications by class and number, with a description of
each. Originally published in *The Equinox* I (10) in 1913 and
subsequently revised, it serves as the authoritative index of what each
liber is and where it stands in the system.

The third source is James A. Eshelman's *The Mystical and Magical
System of the A∴A∴* (College of Thelema, 2000), a modern study that
organizes the grade-by-grade curriculum into a practical working
format, drawing on all available primary documents—including Liber
XIII (*Graduum Montis Abiegni*), *One Star in Sight*, and the 1919
"Præmonstrance" and "Curriculum"—to clarify which texts belong to

which grade when the official sources are ambiguous or incomplete. Where these three authorities agree, the assignment is straightforward. Where they differ, editorial judgment has been exercised, and such choices are noted where relevant.

These compilations contain only the *libri* themselves. Each grade of the A∴A∴ also prescribes a broader reading list that may include works by other authors—the *Tao Te Ching*, the *Dhammapada*, Patanjali's *Yoga Sutras*, the writings of David Hume, and others—as well as practices to be carried out under the guidance of a superior. Those external readings are not reproduced here. The present volumes are intended as a practical convenience: a way to keep the core instructional texts of a given grade together, in order, and in a readable form, so that the student may study them without hunting through scattered and sometimes unreliable sources.

The texts themselves carry a classification that the reader should understand.

Class A publications are writings received in a state of illumination, held to be supernally inspired, and not to be altered so much as by the style of a letter.

Class B writings are works of scholarship or informed exposition by individual adepts.

Class C is material suggested by A∴A∴ theory but not official.

Class D publications are the official rituals, instructions, and examination papers of the Order, setting out what is to be done and how.

Class E consists of public manifestos and other broadsheets. Some publications are composite, pertaining to more than one class.

The reader will find texts of several classes within each volume, and should approach them accordingly: a Class A text demands a different quality of attention than a Class D instruction on how to perform a ritual, though both are essential to the work.

TABLE OF CONTENTS

LIBER AL

VEL LEGIS

SVB FIGVRÂ

CCXX

AS DELIVERED

BY XCIII = 418

VNTO

DCLXVI

V

A∴A∴

CHAPTER I

1. Had! The manifestation of Nuit.

2. The unveiling of the company of heaven.

3. Every man and every woman is a star.

4. Every number is infinite; there is no difference.

5. Help me, o warrior lord of Thebes, in my unveiling before the Children of men!

6. Be thou Hadit, my secret centre, my heart & my tongue!

7. Behold! it is revealed by Aiwass the minister of Hoor-paar-kraat.

8. The Khabs is in the Khu, not the Khu in the Khabs.

9. Worship then the Khabs, and behold my light shed over you!

10. Let my servants be few & secret: they shall rule the many & the known.

11. These are fools that men adore; both their Gods & their men are fools.

12. Come forth, o children, under the stars, & take your fill of love!

13. I am above you and in you. My ecstasy is in yours. My joy is to see your joy. Above, the gemmèd azure is The naked splendour of Nuit; She bends in ecstasy to kiss The secret ardours of Hadit.

The wingèd globe, the starry blue, Are mine, O Ankh-af-na-khonsu!Now ye shall know that the chosen priest & apostle of infinite space is the prince-priest the Beast; and in his woman called the Scarlet Woman is all power given. They shall gather my children into their fold: they shall bring the glory of the stars into the hearts of men.

14. For he is ever a sun, and she a moon. But to him is the winged secret flame, and to her the stooping starlight.

15. But ye are not so chosen.

16. Burn upon their brows, o splendrous serpent!

17. O azure-lidded woman, bend upon them!

18. The key of the rituals is in the secret word which I have given unto him.

19. With the God & the Adorer I am nothing: they do not see me. They are as upon the earth; I am Heaven, and there is no other God than me, and my lord Hadit.

20. Now, therefore, I am known to ye by my name Nuit, and to him by a secret name which I will give him when at last he knoweth me. Since I am Infinite Space, and the Infinite Stars thereof, do ye also thus. Bind nothing! Let there be no difference made among you between any one thing & any other thing; for thereby there cometh hurt.

21. But whoso availeth in this, let him be the chief of all!

22. I am Nuit, and my word is six and fifty.

23. Divide, add, multiply, and understand.

24. Then saith the prophet and slave of the beauteous one: Who am I, and what shall be the sign? So she answered him, bending down, a lambent flame of blue, all-touching, all penetrant, her lovely hands upon the black earth, & her lithe body arched for love, and her soft feet not hurting the little flowers: Thou knowest! And the sign shall be my ecstasy, the consciousness of the continuity of existence, the omnipresence of my body.

25. Then the priest answered & said unto the Queen of Space, kissing her lovely brows, and the dew of her light bathing his whole body in a sweet-smelling perfume of sweat: O Nuit, continuous one of Heaven, let it be ever thus; that men speak not of Thee as One but as None; and let them speak not of thee at all, since thou art continuous!

26. None, breathed the light, faint & faery, of the stars, and two.

27. For I am divided for love's sake, for the chance of union.

28. This is the creation of the world, that the pain of division is as nothing, and the joy of dissolution all.

29. For these fools of men and their woes care not thou at all! They feel little; what is, is balanced by weak joys; but ye are my chosen ones.

30. Obey my prophet! follow out the ordeals of my knowledge!

seek me only! Then the joys of my love will redeem ye from all pain. This is so: I swear it by the vault of my body; by my sacred heart and tongue; by all I can give, by all I desire of ye all.

31. Then the priest fell into a deep trance or swoon, & said unto the Queen of Heaven; Write unto us the ordeals; write unto us the rituals; write unto us the law!

32. But she said: the ordeals I write not: the rituals shall be half known and half concealed: the Law is for all.

33. This that thou writest is the threefold book of Law.

34. My scribe Ankh-af-na-khonsu, the priest of the princes, shall not in one letter change this book; but lest there be folly, he shall comment thereupon by the wisdom of Ra-Hoor-Khu-it.

35. Also the mantras and spells; the obeah and the wanga; the work of the wand and the work of the sword; these he shall learn and teach.

36. He must teach; but he may make severe the ordeals.

37. The word of the Law is θέλημα.

38. Who calls us Thelemites will do no wrong, if he look but close into the word. For there are therein Three Grades, the Hermit, and the Lover, and the man of Earth. Do what thou wilt shall be the whole of the Law.

39. The word of Sin is Restriction. O man! refuse not thy wife, if she will! O lover, if thou wilt, depart! There is no bond that can

unite the divided but love: all else is a curse. Accurséd! Accurséd be it to the æons! Hell.

40. Let it be that state of manyhood bound and loathing. So with thy all; thou hast no right but to do thy will.

41. Do that, and no other shall say nay.

42. For pure will, unassuaged of purpose, delivered from the lust of result, is every way perfect.

43. The Perfect and the Perfect are one Perfect and not two; nay, are none!

44. Nothing is a secret key of this law. Sixty-one the Jews call it; I call it eight, eighty, four hundred & eighteen.

45. But they have the half: unite by thine art so that all disappear.

46. My prophet is a fool with his one, one, one; are they not the Ox, and none by the Book?

47. Abrogate are all rituals, all ordeals, all words and signs. Ra-Hoor-Khuit hath taken his seat in the East at the Equinox of the Gods; and let Asar be with Isa, who also are one. But they are not of me. Let Asar be the adorant, Isa the sufferer; Hoor in his secret name and splendour is the Lord initiating.

48. There is a word to say about the Hierophantic task. Behold! there are three ordeals in one, and it may be given in three ways. The gross must pass through fire; let the fine be tried in intellect, and the lofty chosen ones in the highest. Thus ye have star & star, system & system; let not one know well the other!

49. There are four gates to one palace; the floor of that palace is of silver and gold; lapis lazuli & jasper are there; and all rare scents; jasmine & rose, and the emblems of death. Let him enter in turn or at once the four gates; let him stand on the floor of the palace. Will he not sink? Amn. Ho! warrior, if thy servant sink? But there are means and means. Be goodly therefore: dress ye all in fine apparel; eat rich foods and drink sweet wines and wines that foam! Also, take your fill and will of love as ye will, when, where and with whom ye will! But always unto me.

50. If this be not aright; if ye confound the space-marks, saying: They are one; or saying, They are many; if the ritual be not ever unto me: then expect the direful judgements of Ra Hoor Khuit!

51. This shall regenerate the world, the little world my sister, my heart & my tongue, unto whom I send this kiss. Also, o scribe and prophet, though thou be of the princes, it shall not assuage thee nor absolve thee. But ecstasy be thine and joy of earth: ever To me! To me!

52. Change not as much as the style of a letter; for behold! thou, o prophet, shalt not behold all these mysteries hidden therein.

53. The child of thy bowels, he shall behold them.

54. Expect him not from the East, nor from the West; for from no expected house cometh that child. Aum! All words are sacred

and all prophets true; save only that they understand a little; solve the first half of the equation, leave the second unattacked. But thou hast all in the clear light, and some, though not all, in the dark.

55. Invoke me under my stars! Love is the law, love under will. Nor let the fools mistake love; for there are love and love. There is the dove, and there is the serpent. Choose ye well! He, my prophet, hath chosen, knowing the law of the fortress, and the great mystery of the House of God. All these old letters of my Book are aright; but x is not the Star. This also is secret: my prophet shall reveal it to the wise.

56. I give unimaginable joys on earth: certainty, not faith, while in life, upon death; peace unutterable, rest, ecstasy; nor do I demand aught in sacrifice.

57. My incense is of resinous woods & gums; and there is no blood therein: because of my hair the trees of Eternity.

58. My number is 11, as all their numbers who are of us. The Five Pointed Star, with a Circle in the Middle, & the circle is Red. My colour is black to the blind, but the blue & gold are seen of the seeing. Also I have a secret glory for them that love me.

59. But to love me is better than all things: if under the night-stars in the desert thou presently burnest mine incense before me, invoking me with a pure heart, and the Serpent flame therein,

thou shalt come a little to lie in my bosom. For one kiss wilt thou then be willing to give all; but whoso gives one particle of dust shall lose all in that hour. Ye shall gather goods and store of women and spices; ye shall wear rich jewels; ye shall exceed the nations of the earth in splendour & pride; but always in the love of me, and so shall ye come to my joy. I charge you earnestly to come before me in a single robe, and covered with a rich headdress. I love you! I yearn to you! Pale or purple, veiled or voluptuous, I who am all pleasure and purple, and drunkenness of the innermost sense, desire you. Put on the wings, and arouse the coiled splendour within you: come unto me!

60. At all my meetings with you shall the priestess say—and her eyes shall burn with desire as she stands bare and rejoicing in my secret temple—To me! To me! calling forth the flame of the hearts of all in her love-chant.

61. Sing the rapturous love-song unto me! Burn to me perfumes! Wear to me jewels! Drink to me, for I love you! I love you!

62. I am the blue-lidded daughter of Sunset; I am the naked brilliance of the voluptuous night-sky.

63. To me! To me!

64. The Manifestation of Nuit is at an end.

CHAPTER II

1. Nu! the hiding of Hadit.

2. Come! all ye, and learn the secret that hath not yet been revealed. I, Hadit, am the complement of Nu, my bride. I am not extended, and Khabs is the name of my House.

3. In the sphere I am everywhere the centre, as she, the circumference, is nowhere found.

4. Yet she shall be known & I never.

5. Behold! the rituals of the old time are black. Let the evil ones be cast away; let the good ones be purged by the prophet! Then shall this Knowledge go aright.

6. I am the flame that burns in every heart of man, and in the core of every star. I am Life, and the giver of Life, yet therefore is the knowledge of me the knowledge of death.

7. I am the Magician and the Exorcist. I am the axle of the wheel, and the cube in the circle. "Come unto me" is a foolish word: for it is I that go.

8. Who worshipped Heru-pa-kraath have worshipped me; ill, for I am the worshipper.

9. Remember all ye that existence is pure joy; that all the sorrows are but as shadows; they pass & are done; but there is that which remains.

10. O prophet! thou hast ill will to learn this writing.

11. I see thee hate the hand & the pen; but I am stronger.

12. Because of me in Thee which thou knewest not.

13. for why? Because thou wast the knower, and me.

14. Now let there be a veiling of this shrine: now let the light devour men and eat them up with blindness!

15. For I am perfect, being Not; and my number is nine by the fools; but with the just I am eight, and one in eight: which is vital, for I am none indeed. The Empress and the King are not of me; for there is a further secret.

16. I am The Empress & the Hierophant. Thus eleven, as my bride is eleven.

17.Hear me, ye people of sighing! The sorrows of pain and regret
   Are left to the dead and the dying, The folk that not know me as
   yet.

18. These are dead, these fellows; they feel not. We are not for the poor and sad: the lords of the earth are our kinsfolk.

19. Is God to live in a dog? No! but the highest are of us. They shall rejoice, our chosen; who sorroweth is not of us.

20. Beauty and strength, leaping laughter and delicious languor, force and fire, are of us.

21. We have nothing with the outcast and the unfit: let them die in their misery. For they feel not. Compassion is the vice of kings: stamp down the wretched & the weak: this is the law of the strong: this is our law and the joy of the world. Think not, o king,

upon that lie: That Thou Must Die: verily, thou shalt not die, but live. Now let it be understood: If the body of the King dissolve, he shall remain in pure ecstasy for ever. Nuit! Hadit! Ra-Hoor-Khuit! The Sun, Strength & Sight, Light; these are for the servants of the Star & the Snake.

22. I am the Snake that giveth Knowledge & Delight and bright glory, and stir the hearts of men with drunkenness. To worship me take wine and strange drugs whereof I will tell my prophet, & be drunk thereof! They shall not harm ye at all. It is a lie, this folly against self. The exposure of innocence is a lie. Be strong, o man! lust, enjoy all things of sense and rapture: fear not that any God shall deny thee for this.

23. I am alone: there is no God where I am.

24. Behold! these be grave mysteries; for there are also of my friends who be hermits. Now, think not to find them in the forest or on the mountain; but in beds of purple, caressed by magnificent beasts of women with large limbs, and fire and light in their eyes, and masses of flaming hair about them; there shall ye find them. Ye shall see them at rule, at victorious armies, at all the joy; and there shall be in them a joy a million times greater than this. Beware, lest any force another, King against King! Love one another with burning hearts; on the low men trample in the fierce lust of your pride, in the day of your wrath.

25. Ye are against the people, O my chosen!

26. I am the secret Serpent coiled about to spring: in my coiling there is joy. If I lift up my head, I and my Nuit are one. If I droop down mine head, and shoot forth venom, then is rapture of the earth, and I and the earth are one.

27. There is great danger in me; for who doth not understand these runes shall make a great miss. He shall fall down into the pit called Because, and there he shall perish with the dogs of Reason.

28. Now a curse upon Because and his kin!

29. May Because be accursèd for ever!

30. If Will stops and cries Why, invoking Because, then Will stops & does nought.

31. If Power asks why, then is Power weakness.

32. Also reason is a lie; for there is a factor infinite & unknown; & all their words are skew-wise.

33. Enough of Because! Be he damned for a dog!

34. But ye, o my people, rise up & awake!

35. Let the rituals be rightly performed with joy & beauty!

36. There are rituals of the elements and feasts of the times.

37. A feast for the first night of the Prophet and his Bride!

38. A feast for the three days of the writing of the Book of the Law.

39. A feast for Tahuti and the child of the Prophet—secret, O

Prophet!

40. A feast for the Supreme Ritual, and a feast for the Equinox of the Gods.

41. A feast for fire and a feast for water; a feast for life and a greater feast for death!

42. A feast every day in your hearts in the joy of my rapture!

43. A feast every night unto Nu, and the pleasure of uttermost delight!

44. Aye! feast! rejoice! there is no dread hereafter. There is the dissolution, and eternal ecstasy in the kisses of Nu.

45. There is death for the dogs.

46. Dost thou fail? Art thou sorry? Is fear in thine heart?

47. Where I am these are not.

48. Pity not the fallen! I never knew them. I am not for them. I console not: I hate the consoled & the consoler.

49. I am unique & conqueror. I am not of the slaves that perish. Be they damned and dead! Amen. (This is of the 4: there is a fifth who is invisible, & therein am I as a babe in an egg.)

50. Blue am I and gold in the light of my bride: but the red gleam is in my eyes; & my spangles are purple & green.

51. Purple beyond purple: it is the light higher than eyesight.

52. There is a veil: that veil is black. It is the veil of the modest woman; it is the veil of sorrow, & the pall of death: this is none of

me. Tear down that lying spectre of the centuries: veil not your vices in virtuous words: these vices are my service; ye do well, & I will reward you here and hereafter.

53. Fear not, o prophet, when these words are said, thou shalt not be sorry. Thou art emphatically my chosen; and blessed are the eyes that thou shalt look upon with gladness. But I will hide thee in a mask of sorrow: they that see thee shall fear thou art fallen: but I lift thee up.

54. Nor shall they who cry aloud their folly that thou meanest nought avail; thou shalt reveal it: thou availest: they are the slaves of because: They are not of me. The stops as thou wilt; the letters? change them not in style or value!

55. Thou shalt obtain the order & value of the English Alphabet; thou shalt find new symbols to attribute them unto.

56. Begone! ye mockers; even though ye laugh in my honour ye shall laugh not long: then when ye are sad know that I have forsaken you.

57. He that is righteous shall be righteous still; he that is filthy shall be filthy still.

58. Yea! deem not of change: ye shall be as ye are, & not other. Therefore the kings of the earth shall be Kings for ever: the slaves shall serve. There is none that shall be cast down or lifted up: all is ever as it was. Yet there are masked ones my servants: it

may be that yonder beggar is a King. A King may choose his garment as he will: there is no certain test: but a beggar cannot hide his poverty.

59. Beware therefore! Love all, lest perchance is a King concealed! Say you so? Fool! If he be a King, thou canst not hurt him.

60. Therefore strike hard & low, and to hell with them, master!

61. There is a light before thine eyes, o prophet, a light undesired, most desirable.

62. I am uplifted in thine heart; and the kisses of the stars rain hard upon thy body.

63. Thou art exhaust in the voluptuous fullness of the inspiration; the expiration is sweeter than death, more rapid and laughterful than a caress of Hell's own worm.

64. Oh! thou art overcome: we are upon thee; our delight is all over thee: hail! hail: prophet of Nu! prophet of Had! prophet of Ra-Hoor-Khu! Now rejoice! now come in our splendour & rapture! Come in our passionate peace, & write sweet words for the Kings!

65. I am the Master: thou art the Holy Chosen One.

66. Write, & find ecstasy in writing! Work, & be our bed in working! Thrill with the joy of life & death! Ah! thy death shall be lovely: whoso seeth it shall be glad. Thy death shall be the seal

of the promise of our agelong love. Come! lift up thine heart & rejoice! We are one; we are none.

67. Hold! Hold! Bear up in thy rapture; fall not in swoon of the excellent kisses!

68. Harder! Hold up thyself! Lift thine head! breathe not so deep—die!

69. Ah! Ah! What do I feel? Is the word exhausted?

70. There is help & hope in other spells. Wisdom says: be strong! Then canst thou bear more joy. Be not animal; refine thy rapture! If thou drink, drink by the eight and ninety rules of art: if thou love, exceed by delicacy; and if thou do aught joyous, let there be subtlety therein!

71. But exceed! exceed!

72. Strive ever to more! and if thou art truly mine—and doubt it not, an if thou art ever joyous!—death is the crown of all.

73. Ah! Ah! Death! Death! thou shalt long for death. Death is forbidden, o man, unto thee.

74. The length of thy longing shall be the strength of its glory. He that lives long & desires death much is ever the King among the Kings.

75. Aye! listen to the numbers & the words:

76. 4 6 3 8 A B K 2 4 A L G M O R 3 Y X 24 89 R P S T O V A L. What meaneth this, o prophet? Thou knowest not; nor shalt

thou know ever. There cometh one to follow thee: he shall expound it. But remember, o chosen one, to be me; to follow the love of Nu in the star-lit heaven; to look forth upon men, to tell them this glad word.

77. O be thou proud and mighty among men!

78. Lift up thyself! for there is none like unto thee among men or among Gods! Lift up thyself, o my prophet, thy stature shall surpass the stars. They shall worship thy name, foursquare, mystic, wonderful, the number of the man; and the name of thy house 418.

79. The end of the hiding of Hadit; and blessing & worship to the prophet of the lovely Star!

CHAPTER III

1. Abrahadabra; the reward of Ra Hoor Khut.

2. There is division hither homeward; there is a word not known. Spelling is defunct; all is not aught. Beware! Hold! Raise the spell of Ra-Hoor-Khuit!

3. Now let it be first understood that I am a god of War and of Vengeance. I shall deal hardly with them.

4. Choose ye an island!

5. Fortify it!

6. Dung it about with enginery of war!

7. I will give you a war-engine.

8. With it ye shall smite the peoples; and none shall stand before you.

9. Lurk! Withdraw! Upon them! this is the Law of the Battle of Conquest: thus shall my worship be about my secret house.

10. Get the stélé of revealing itself; set it in thy secret temple—and that temple is already aright disposed—& it shall be your Kiblah for ever. It shall not fade, but miraculous colour shall come back to it day after day. Close it in locked glass for a proof to the world.

11. This shall be your only proof. I forbid argument. Conquer! That is enough. I will make easy to you the abstraction from the ill-ordered house in the Victorious City. Thou shalt thyself convey it with worship, o prophet, though thou likest it not. Thou shalt have danger & trouble. Ra-Hoor-Khu is with thee. Worship me with fire & blood; worship me with swords & with spears. Let the woman be girt with a sword before me: let blood flow to my name. Trample down the Heathen; be upon them, o warrior, I will give you of their flesh to eat!

12. Sacrifice cattle, little and big: after a child.

13. But not now.

14. Ye shall see that hour, o blessèd Beast, and thou the Scarlet Concubine of his desire!

15. Ye shall be sad thereof.

16. Deem not too eagerly to catch the promises; fear not to undergo the curses. Ye, even ye, know not this meaning all.

17. Fear not at all; fear neither men nor Fates, nor gods, nor anything. Money fear not, nor laughter of the folk folly, nor any other power in heaven or upon the earth or under the earth. Nu is your refuge as Hadit your light; and I am the strength, force, vigour, of your arms.

18. Mercy let be off: damn them who pity! Kill and torture; spare not; be upon them!

19. That stélé they shall call the Abomination of Desolation; count well its name, & it shall be to you as 718.

20. Why? Because of the fall of Because, that he is not there again.

21. Set up my image in the East: thou shalt buy thee an image which I will show thee, especial, not unlike the one thou knowest. And it shall be suddenly easy for thee to do this.

22. The other images group around me to support me: let all be worshipped, for they shall cluster to exalt me. I am the visible object of worship; the others are secret; for the Beast & his Bride are they: and for the winners of the Ordeal x. What is this? Thou shalt know.

23. For perfume mix meal & honey & thick leavings of red wine: then oil of Abramelin and olive oil, and afterward soften &

smooth down with rich fresh blood.

24. The best blood is of the moon, monthly: then the fresh blood of a child, or dropping from the host of heaven: then of enemies; then of the priest or of the worshippers: last of some beast, no matter what.

25. This burn: of this make cakes & eat unto me. This hath also another use; let it be laid before me, and kept thick with perfumes of your orison: it shall become full of beetles as it were and creeping things sacred unto me.

26. These slay, naming your enemies; & they shall fall before you.

27. Also these shall breed lust & power of lust in you at the eating thereof.

28. Also ye shall be strong in war.

29. Moreover, be they long kept, it is better; for they swell with my force. All before me.

30. My altar is of open brass work: burn thereon in silver or gold!

31. There cometh a rich man from the West who shall pour his gold upon thee.

32. From gold forge steel!

33. Be ready to fly or to smite!

34. But your holy place shall be untouched throughout the centuries: though with fire and sword it be burnt down & shattered, yet an invisible house there standeth, and shall stand

until the fall of the Great Equinox; when Hrumachis shall arise and the double-wanded one assume my throne and place. Another prophet shall arise, and bring fresh fever from the skies; another woman shall awake the lust & worship of the Snake; another soul of God and beast shall mingle in the globèd priest; another sacrifice shall stain the tomb; another king shall reign; and blessing no longer be poured To the Hawk-headed mystical Lord!

35. The half of the word of Heru-ra-ha, called Hoor-pa-kraat and Ra-Hoor-Khut.

36. Then said the prophet unto the God:

37. I adore thee in the song—

> *I am the Lord of Thebes, and I The*
>
> *inspired forth-speaker of Mentu;*
>
> *For me unveils the veilèd sky, The*
>
> *self-slain Ankh-af-na-khonsu*
>
> *Whose words are truth. I invoke, I greet Thy*
>
> *presence, O Ra-Hoor-Khuit!*
>
> *Unity uttermost showed!*
>
> *I adore the might of Thy breath, Supreme*
>
> *and terrible God,*
>
> *Who makest the gods and death To*
>
> *tremble before Thee:—*

38. So that thy light is in me; & its red flame is as a sword in my hand to push thy order. There is a secret door that I shall make to establish thy way in all the quarters, (these are the adorations, as thou hast written), as it is said:

39. All this and a book to say how thou didst come hither and a reproduction of this ink and paper for ever—for in it is the word secret & not only in the English—and thy comment upon this the Book of the Law shall be printed beautifully in red ink and black upon beautiful paper made by hand; and to each man and woman that thou meetest, were it but to dine or to drink at them, it is the Law to give. Then they shall chance to abide in this bliss or no; it is no odds. Do this quickly!

40. But the work of the comment? That is easy; and Hadit burning in thy heart shall make swift and secure thy pen.

41. Establish at thy Kaaba a clerk-house: all must be done well and with business way.

42. The ordeals thou shalt oversee thyself, save only the blind ones. Refuse none, but thou shalt know & destroy the traitors. I am Ra-Hoor-Khuit; and I am powerful to protect my servant. Success is thy proof: argue not; convert not; talk not overmuch! Them that seek to entrap thee, to overthrow thee, them attack without pity or quarter; & destroy them utterly. Swift as a trodden serpent turn and strike! Be thou yet deadlier than he! Drag down their souls to awful torment: laugh at their fear: spit upon them!

43. Let the Scarlet Woman beware! If pity and compassion and tenderness visit her heart; if she leave my work to toy with old sweetnesses; then shall my vengeance be known. I will slay me her child: I will alienate her heart: I will cast her out from men: as a shrinking and despised harlot shall she crawl through dusk wet streets, and die cold and an-hungered.

44. But let her raise herself in pride! Let her follow me in my way! Let her work the work of wickedness! Let her kill her heart! Let her be loud and adulterous! Let her be covered with jewels, and rich garments, and let her be shameless before all men!

45. Then will I lift her to pinnacles of power: then will I breed from her a child mightier than all the kings of the earth. I will fill her with joy: with my force shall she see & strike at the worship of Nu: she shall achieve Hadit.

46. I am the warrior Lord of the Forties: the Eighties cower before me, & are abased. I will bring you to victory & joy: I will be at your arms in battle & ye shall delight to slay. Success is your proof; courage is your armour; go on, go on, in my strength; & ye shall turn not back for any!

47. This book shall be translated into all tongues: but always with the original in the writing of the Beast; for in the chance shape of the letters and their position to one another: in these are mysteries that no Beast shall divine. Let him not seek to try: but one cometh after him, whence I say not, who shall discover the Key of it all. Then this line drawn is a key: then this circle squared in its failure is a key also. And Abrahadabra. It shall be his child &

that strangely. Let him not seek after this; for thereby alone can he fall from it.

48. Now this mystery of the letters is done, and I want to go on to the holier place.

49. I am in a secret fourfold word, the blasphemy against all gods of men.

50. Curse them! Curse them! Curse them!

51. With my Hawk's head I peck at the eyes of Jesus as he hangs upon the cross.

52. I flap my wings in the face of Mohammed & blind him.

53. With my claws I tear out the flesh of the Indian and the Buddhist, Mongol and Din.

54. Bahlasti! Ompehda! I spit on your crapulous creeds.

55. Let Mary inviolate be torn upon wheels: for her sake let all chaste women be utterly despised among you!

56. Also for beauty's sake and love's!

57. Despise also all cowards; professional soldiers who dare not fight, but play; all fools despise!

58. But the keen and the proud, the royal and the lofty; ye are brothers!

59. As brothers fight ye!

60. There is no law beyond Do what thou wilt.

61. There is an end of the word of the God enthroned in Ra's seat, lightening the girders of the soul.

62. To Me do ye reverence! to me come ye through tribulation of ordeal, which is bliss.

63. The fool readeth this Book of the Law, and its comment; & he understandeth it not.

64. Let him come through the first ordeal, & it will be to him as silver.

65. Through the second, gold.

66. Through the third, stones of precious water.

67. Through the fourth, ultimate sparks of the intimate fire.

68. Yet to all it shall seem beautiful. Its enemies who say not so, are mere liars.

69. There is success.

70. I am the Hawk-Headed Lord of Silence & of Strength; my nemyss shrouds the night-blue sky.

71. Hail! ye twin warriors about the pillars of the world! for your time is nigh at hand.

72. I am the Lord of the Double Wand of Power; the wand of the Force of Coph Nia—but my left hand is empty, for I have crushed an Universe; & nought remains.

73. Paste the sheets from right to left and from top to bottom: then behold!

74. There is a splendour in my name hidden and glorious, as the

sun of midnight is ever the son.

75. The ending of the words is the Word Abrahadabra.

The Book of the Law is Written

and Concealed.

Aum. Ha.

THE COMMENT

Do what thou wilt shall be the whole of the Law.

The study of this Book is forbidden. It is wise to destroy this copy after the first reading.

Whosoever disregards this does so at his own risk and peril. These are most dire.

Those who discuss the contents of this Book are to be shunned by all, as centres of pestilence.

All questions of the Law are to be decided only by appeal to my writings, each for himself.

There is no law beyond Do what thou wilt.

Love is the law, love under will.

The priest of the princes,

Ankh-af-na-khonsu

LIBER

TRIGRAMMATON

SVB FIGVRÂ XXVII

BEING THE BOOK
OF THE TRIGRAMS
OF THE MUTATIONS
OF THE TAO
WITH THE YIN AND THE YANG

V

A∴A∴

Publication in Class A

The full knowledge of the interpretation of this book is concealed from all.

The Practicus must nevertheless acquire a copy and throughly acquaint himself with the contents, and commit them to memory.

Here is Nothing under its three forms. It is not, yet informeth all things.

Now cometh the glory of the Single One, as an imperfection and stain. But by the Weak One the Mother was it equilibrated.

Also the purity was divided by Strength, the force of the Demiurge.

And the Cross was formulated in the Universe that as yet was not.

But now the Imperfection became manifest, presiding over the fading of perfection.

Also the Woman arose, and veiled the Upper Heaven with her body of stars.

Now then a giant arose, of terrible strength; and asserted the Spirit in a secret rite.

And the Master of the Temple balancing all things arose; his stature was above the Heaven and below Earth and Hell.

Against him the Brothers of the Left-hand Path, confusing the symbols. They concealed their horror [in this symbol]; for in truth they were

The master flamed forth as a star and set a guard of Water in every Abyss.

Also certain secret ones concealed the Light of Purity in themselves, protecting it from the Persecutions.

Likewise also did certain sons and daughters of Hermes and of Aphrodite, more openly.

But the Enemy confused them. They pretended to conceal that Light, that they might betray it, and profane it.

Yet certain holy nuns concealed the secret in songs upon the lyre.

Now did the Horror of Time pervert all things, hiding the Purity with a loathsome thing, a thing unnameable

Yea, and there arose sensualists upon the firmament, as a foul stain of storm upon the sky.

And the Black Brothers raised their heads; yea, they unveiled themselves without shame or fear.

Also there rose up a soul of filth and of weakness, and it corrupted all the rule of the Tao.

Then only was Heaven established to bear sway; for only in the lowest corruption is form manifest.

Also did Heaven manifest in violent light.

And in soft light.

Then were the waters gathered together from the heaven.

And a crust of earth concealed the core of flame.

Around the globe gathered the wide air.

And men began to light fires upon the

earth.

Therefore was the end of it sorrow; yet in that sorrow a sixfold

star of glory whereby they might see to return unto the stainless

Abode; yea, unto the Stainless Abode.

LIBER

DCCCXIII

VEL

ARARITA

SVB FIGVRÂ

DLXX

V

A∴A∴

The full knowledge of the interpretation of this book is concealed from all. The Philosophus must nevertheless acquire a copy and throughly acquaint himself with the contents. He must commit one chapter to memory.

I

א

0. O my God! One is Thy Beginning! One is Thy Spirit, and Thy Permutation One!

1. Let me extol Thy perfections before men.

2. In the Image of a Sixfold Star that flameth across the Vault inane, let me re-veil Thy perfections.

3. Thou hast appeared unto me as an agèd God, a venerable God, the Lord of Time, bearing a sharp sickle.

4. Thou hast appeared unto me as a jocund and ruddy God, full of Majesty, a King, a Father in his prime. Thou didst bear the sceptre of the Universe, crowned with the Wheel of the Spirit.

5. Thou hast appeared unto me with sword and spear, a warrior God in flaming armour among Thine horsemen.

6. Thou hast appeared unto me as a young and brilliant God, a god of music and beauty, even as a young god in his strength, playing upon the lyre.

7. Thou has appeared unto me as the white foam of Ocean gathered into limbs whiter than the foam, the limbs of a miracle of women, as a goddess of extreme love, bearing the girdle of gold.

8. Thou hast appeared unto me as a young boy mischievous and lovely, with Thy winged globe and its serpents set upon a staff.

9. Thou hast appeared to me as an huntress among Thy dogs, as a goddess virginal chaste, as a moon among the faded oaks of the wood of years.

10. But I was deceived by none of these. All these I cast aside, crying: Begone! So that all these faded from my vision.

11. Also I welded together the Flaming Star and the Sixfold Star in the forge of my soul, and behold! a new star 418 that is above all these.

12. Yet even so was I not deceived; for the crown hath twelve rays.

13. And these twelve rays are one.

II

ר

0. Now then I saw things averse and evil; and they were not, even as Thou art Not.

1. I saw the twin heads that even battle against one another, so that all their thought is a confusion. I saw Thee in these.

2. I saw the darkeners of wisdom, like black apes chattering vile nonsense. I saw Thee in these.

3. I saw the devouring mothers of Hell, that eat up their children—O ye that are without understanding! I saw Thee in these.

4. I saw the merciless and unmajestic like harpies, tearing their foul food. I saw Thee in these.

5. I saw the burning ones, giants like volcanoes belching out the black vomit of fire and smoke in their fury. I saw Thee in these.

6. I saw the petty, the quarrelsome, the selfish,—they were like men, O Lord, they were like men, O Lord, they were even like unto men. I saw Thee in these.

7. I saw the ravens of death, that flew with hoarse cries upon the carrion earth. I saw Thee in these.

8. I saw the lying spirits like frogs upon the earth, and upon the water, and upon the treacherous metal that corrodeth all things and abideth not. I saw Thee in these.

9. I saw the obscene ones, bull-men linked in the abyss of putrefaction, that gnawed each other's tounges for pain. I saw Thee in these.

10. I saw the Woman. O my God, I beheld the image thereof, even as a lovely shape that concealeth a black monkey, even as a figure that draweth with her hands small images of men down into hell. I saw her from the head to the navel a woman, from the navel to the feet of her a man. I saw Thee even in her.

11. For mine was the keyword to the Closed Palace 418 and mine the reins of the Chariot of the Sphinxes, black and white. But I was not deceived by anything of all these things.

12. For I expanded it by my subtlety into Twelve Rays of the Crown.

13. And these twelve rays were One.

III

א

0. Say thou that He God is one; God is the Everlasting One; nor hath He any Equal, or any Son, or any Companion. Nothing shall stand before His face.

1. Even for five hundred and eleven times nightly for one and forty days did I cry aloud unto the Lord the affirmation of His Unity.

2. Also did I glorify His wisdom, whereby He made the worlds.

3. Yea, I praised Him for His intelligible essence, whereby the universe became light.

4. I did thank Him for his manifold mercy; I did worship

His magnificence and majesty.

5. I trembled before His might.

6. I delighted in the Harmony and Beauty of his Essence.

7. In His Victory I pursued His enemies; yea I drave them down the steep; I thundered after them into the utmost abyss; yea, therein I partook of the glory of my Lord.

8. His Splendour shone upon me; I adored his adorable splendour.

9. I rested myself, admiring the Stability of Him, how the shaking of His Universe, the dissolution of all things, should move Him not.

10. Yea, verily, I the Lord Viceregent of his Kingdom, I, Adonai, who speak unto my servant V.V.V.V.V. did rule and govern in His place.

11. Yet also did I formulate the word of double power in the Voice of the Master, even the word 418.

12. And all these things deceived me not, for I expanded them by my subtlety into the Twelve Rays of the Crown.

13. And these twelve rays were One.

IV

ר

0. Also the little child, the lover of Adonai, even V.V.V.V.V.,

reflecting the glory of Adonai, lifted up his voice and said:

1. Glory to God, and Thanksgiving to God! There is One God alone, and God is exceeding great. He is about us, and there is no strength save in Him the exalted, the great.

2. Thus did V.V.V.V.V. become mad, and wend about naked.

3. And all these things fled away, for he understood them all, that they were but as old rags upon the Divine Perfection.

4. Also he pitied them, that they were but reflections distored.

5. Also he smote them, lest they should bear rule over the just.

6. Also he harmonized them into one picture, beautiful to behold.

7. And having thus conquered them, there was a certain glamour of holiness even in the hollow sphere of outward brilliance.

8. So that all became splendid.

9. And having firmly established them in order and disposition,

10. He proclaimed the perfection, the bride, the delight of God in his creation.

11. But though thus he worked, he tried ever his work by the Star 418.

12. And it deceived him not; for by his subtlety he expanded it all into the Twelve Rays of the Crown.

13. And these twelve rays were One.

V

ר

0. In the place of the cross the indivisible point which hath no points nor part nor magnitude. Nor indeed hath it position, being beyond space. Nor hath it existence in time, for it is beyond Time. Nor hath it cause or effect, seeing that its Universe is infinite every way, and partaketh not of these our conceptions.

1. So wrote οὐ μή the Exempt Adept, and the laughter of the Masters of the Temple abashed him not.

2. Nor was he ashamed, hearing the laughter of the little dogs of hell.

3. For he abode in his place, and his falsehood was truth in his place.

4. The little dogs cannot correct him, for they can do naught but bark.

5. The masters cannot correct him, for they say: Come and see.

6. And I came and saw, even I, Perdurabo, the Philosophus of the Outer College.

7. Yea, even I the man beheld this wonder.

8. And I could not deliver it unto myself.

9. That which established me is invisible and unknowable in its essence.

10. Only they who know IT may be known.

11. For they have the genius of the mighty sword 418.

12. And they are not deceived by any of these things; for by their subtlety do they expand them all into the Twelve Rays of the Crown.

13. And these twelve rays are One.

VI

ת

0. Deeper and deeper into the mire of things! Farther and farther into the never-ended Expansion of the Abyss.

1. The great goddess that bendeth over the Universe is my mistress; I am the winged globe at her heart.

2. I contract ever as she ever expandeth.

3. At the end it is all one.

4. Our loves have brought to birth the Father and Creator of all things.

5. He hath established the elements, the æthyr, the air, the water, the earth, and the fire.

6. He hath established the wanderings stars in their courses.

7. He hath ploughed with the seven stars of his Plough, that the Seven might move indeed, yet ever point to the unchanging

One.

8. He hath established the Eight Belts, wherewith he hath girdled the globes.

9. He hath established the Trinity of Triads in all things, forcing fire into fire, and ordering all things in the Stable Abode of the Kings of Ægypt.

10. He hath established His rule in His kingdom.

11. Yet the Father also boweth unto the Power of the Star 418 and thereby

12. In his subtlety He expandeth it all into twelve rays of the Crown.

13. And these twelve rays are One.

VII

א

0. Then in the might of the Lion did I formulate unto myself that holy and formless fire, קדש, which darteth and flasheth through the depths of the Universe.

1. At the touch of the Fire Qadosh the earth melted into a liquor clear as water.

2. At the touch of the Fire Qadosh the water smoked into a lucid air.

3. At the touch of the Fire Qadosh the air ignited, and became Fire.

4. At the touch of the Fire Qadosh, O Lord, the Fire dissipated into Space.

5. At the touch of the Fire Qadosh, O Lord, the Space resolved itself into a profundity of Mind.

6. At the touch of the Fire Qadosh the Mind of the Father was broken up into the brilliance of our Lord the Sun.

7. At the touch of the Fire Qadosh the Brilliance of our Lord was absorbed in the Naught of our Lady of the Body of the Milk of the Stars.

8. Then only was the Fire Qadosh extinguished, when the Enterer was driven back from the threshold,

9. And the Lord of Silence was established upon the Lotus flower.

10. Then was accomplished all that which was to be accomplished.

11. And All and One and Naught were slain in the slaying of the Warrior 418,

12. In the slaying of subtlety that expanded all these things into the Twelve Rays of the Crown,

13. That returned unto One, and beyond One, even unto the vision of the Fool in his folly that chanted the word Ararita, and beyond the Word and the Fool; yea, beyond the Word and the Fool.

LIBER RV

VEL SPIRITVS

SVB FIGVRÂ

CCVI

A∴A∴

Publication in Class D

(Editor's note, 0-1 were not included in earlier versions of Equinox Vol 1-7 and have not been included here.)

2. Let the Zelator observe the current of his breath.

3. Let him investigate the following statements, and prepare a careful record of research.

(a) Certain actions induce the flow of the breath through the right nostril (Pingalā); and, conversely, the flow of the breath through Pingala induces certain actions.

(b) Certain other actions induce the flow of the breath through the left nostril (Idā), and conversely.

(c) Yet a third class of actions induce the flow of the breath through both nostrils at once (suśumnā), and conversely.

(d) The degree of mental and physical activity is interdependent with the distance from the nostrils at which the breath can be felt by the back of the hand.

4. First practice. Let him concentrate his mind upon the act of breathing, saying mentally "The breath flows in," "The breath flows out," and record the results. (This practice may resolve itself into mahāsatipatthāna (vide Liber XXV) or induce samādhi. Whichever occurs should be followed up as the right Ingenium of the Zelator, or the advice of his Practicus, may determine.)

5. Second practice. Prāṇāyāma. This is outlined in "Liber E."

Further, let the Zelator accomplished in these practices endeavour to master a cycle of 10. 20. 40 or even 16. 32. 64. But let this be done gradually and with due caution. And when he is steady and easy both in āsana and prāṇāyāma, let him still further increase the period.

Thus let him investigate these statements which follow:

(a) If prāṇāyāma be properly performed, the body will first of all become covered with sweat. This sweat is different in character from that customarily induced by exertion. If the Practitioner rub this sweat thoroughly into his body, he will greatly strengthen it.

(b) The tendency to perspiration will stop as the practice is continued, and the body become automatically rigid. Describe this rigidity with minute accuracy.

(c) The state of automatic rigidity will develop into a state characterised by violent spasmodic movements of which the Practitioner is unconscious, but of whose result he is aware. This result is that the body hops gently from place to place. After the first two or three occurences of this experience āsana is not lost. The body appears (on another theory) to have lost its weight almost completely, and to be moved by an unknown force.

(d) As a development of this stage, the body rises into the air, and remains there for an appreciably long period, from a second to an hour or more.

Let him further investigate any mental results which occur.

6. Third practice. In order both to economize his time and to develop his powers, let the Zelator practise the deep full breathing which his preliminary exercises will have taught him during his walks. Let him repeat a sacred sentence (mantra) or let him count, in such a way that his footfall beats accurately with the rhythm thereof, as is done in dancing. Then let him practise prāṇāyāma, at first without the kumbhakha, and paying no attention to the nostrils otherwise than to keep them clear. Let him begin by an indrawing of the breath for 4 paces, and a breathing out for 4 paces. Let him increase this gradually to 6.6, 8.8, 12.12, 16.16, and 24.24, or more if he be able. Next let him practise in the proper proportion 4.8, 6.12, 8.16, 12.24 and so on. Then, if he choose, let him recommence the series, adding a gradually increasing period of kumbhakha.

7. Fourth practice. Following on this third practice, let him quicken his mantra and his pace, until the walk develops into a dance. This may also be practised with the ordinary waltz step, using a mantra in three-time, such as ἄπελθον, ἄπελθον, Ἄρτεμι; or ΙΑΩ; ΙΑΩ ΣΑΒΑΩ; in such cases the practice may be combined with devotion to a particular deity; see "Liber 175." For the dance as such it is better to use a mantra of a non-committal character, such as τὸ εἶναι, τὸ καλόν, τὸ ἀγαθόν, or the like.

8. Fifth practice. Let him practice mental concentration during the dance, and investigate the following statement:

(a) The dance becomes independent of the will.

(b) Similar phenomena to those described in 5 (a) (b) (c) (d) occur.

(c) Certain important mental results occur.

9. A note concerning the depth and fullness of the breathing. In all proper expiration, the last possible portion of air should be expelled. In this the muscles of the throat, chest, ribs, and abdomen must be fully employed, and aided by pressing the upper arms into the flanks, and of the head into the thorax.

In all proper inspiration, the last possible portion of air must be drawn into the lungs.

In all proper holding of the breath, the body must remain absolutely still.

Ten minutes of such practice is ample to induce profuse sweating in any place of a temperature of $17°$ C. or over.

The progress of the Zelator in acquiring a depth and fulness of breath should be tested by the respirometer. The exercises should be carefully graduated to avoid overstrain and possible damage to the lungs. This depth and fulness of breath should be kept as much as possible, even in the rapid exercises, with the exception of the sixth practice following.

10. Sixth practice. Let the Zelator breathe as shallowly and rapidly as possible. He should assume the attitude of his moment of greatest expiration, and breathe only with the muscles of his throat. He may also practise lengthening the period between each shallow breathing.

(This may be combined when acquired with concentration on the viśuddhi chakra, i.e. let him fix his mind unwaveringly upon a point in the spine opposite the larynx. ED)

11. Seventh practice. Let the Zelator breathe as deeply and rapidly as possible.

12. Eighth practice. Let the Zelator practice restraint of breathing in the following manner.

At any stage of breathing let him suddenly hold the breath, enduring the need to breathe until it passes, returns, and passes again, and so on until consciousness is lost, either rising into samādhi or similar supernormal condition, or falling to oblivion.

13. Ninth practice. Let him practise the usual forms of prāṇāyāma, but let kumbhakha be used after instead of before expiration. Let him gradually increase the period of this kumbhakha as in the case of the other.

14. A note concerning the conditions of these experiments. The conditions favourable are dry and bracing air, a warm climate, absence of wind, absence of noise, insects, and all other disturbing influences, a retired situation, simple food eaten in

great moderation at the conclusion of the practices of morning and afternoon and on no account before practising. Bodily health is almost essential, and should be most carefully guarded. (See "Liber 185," Task of a Neophyte.) A diligent and tractable disciple, or the Practicus of the Zelator, should aid him in his work. Such a disciple should be noiseless, patient, vigilant, prompt, cheerful, of gentle manner and reverent to his master, intelligent to anticipate his wants, cleanly and gracious, not given to speech, devoted and unselfish. With all this he should be fierce and terrible to strangers and all hostile influences, determined and vigorous, unceasingly vigilant, the guardian of the threshold. It is not desirable that the Zelator should employ any other creature than a man, save in cases of necessity. Yet for some of these purposes a dog will serve, for others a woman. There are also others appointed to serve, but these are not for the Zelator.

15. Tenth practice. Let the Zelator experiment if he will with inhalations of oxygen, nitrous oxide, carbon dioxide, and other gases mixed in small proportion with his air during his practices. These experiments are to be conducted with caution in the presence of a medical man of experience, and they are only useful as facilitating a simulacrum of the results of the proper practices, and thereby enheartening the Zelator.

16. Eleventh practice. Let the Zelator at any time during the

practices, especially during periods of kumbhakha, throw his will utterly toward his Holy Guardian Angel, directing his eyes inward and upward, and turning back his tongue as if to swallow it.

(This latter operation is facilitated by severing the frænum linguæ, which, if done, should be done by a competent surgeon. We do not advise this or any similar method of cheating difficulties. This is, however, harmless.)

In this manner the practice is to be raised from the physical to the spiritual plane, even as the words Ruh, Ruach, Pneuma, Spiritus, Geist, Ghost, and indeed words of almost all languages, have been raised from their physical meaning of wind, air, breath, or movement, to the spiritual plane. (RV is the old root meaning yoni, and hence Wheel (Fr. roue, Lat. rota, wheel), and the corresponding Semitic root means "to go." Similarly Spirit is connected with "spiral."—ED.)

17. Let the Zelator attach no credit to any statements that may have been made throughout the course of this instruction, and reflect that even the counsel which We have given as suitable to the average case may be entirely unsuitable to his own.

PRĀṆĀYĀMA PROPERLY PERFORMED

[*It has been found necessary to show this because students were trying to do it without exertion, and in other ways incorrectly.—ED.*]

- The end of pūraka. The bad definition of the image is due to the spasmodic trembling which accompanies the action.
- Kumbhaka.
- The end of rechaka.

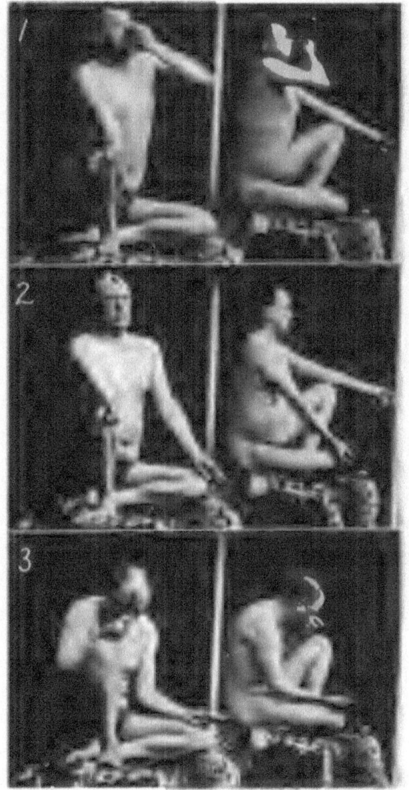

ad definition of the image is due to the

LIBER

תשרב

VIÆ MEMORIÆ

SVB FIGVRÂ

CMXIII

A∴A∴

Publication in Class B

Imprimatur:

N. Fra. A∴A∴

ooo. May be.

oo. [It has not been possible to construct this book on a basis of pure Scepticism. This matters less, as the practice leads to Scepticism, and it may be through it.]

0. This book is not intended to lead to the supreme attainment. On the contrary, its results define the separate being of the Exempt Adept from the rest of the Universe, and discover his relation to that Universe.

1. It is of such importance to the Exempt Adept that We cannot overrate it. Let him in no wise adventure the plunge into the Abyss until he have accomplished this to his most perfectest satisfaction.

2. For in the Abyss no effort is anywise possible. The Abyss is passed by virtue of the mass of the Adept and his Karma. Two forces impel him:

(1) the attraction of Binah, (2) the impulse of his Karma; and the ease and even the safety of his passage depend on the strength and direction of the latter.

3. Should one rashly dare the passage, and take the irrevocable Oath of the Abyss, he might be lost therein through Æons of incalculable agony; he might even be thrown back upon Chesed, with the terrible Karma of failure added to his original imperfection.

4. It is even said that in certain circumstances it is possible to fall altogether from the Tree of Life, and to attain the Towers of the Black Brothers. But We hold that this is not possible for any adept who has truly attained his grade, or even for any man who has really sought to help humanity even for a single second, and that although his aspiration have been impure through vanity or any similar imperfection.

5. Let the Adept who finds the result of these meditations unsatisfactory refuse the Oath of the Abyss, and live so that his Karma gains strength and direction suitable to the task at some future period.

6. Memory is essential to the individual consciousness; otherwise the mind were but a blank sheet on which shadows are cast. But we see that not only does the mind retain impressions, but that it is so constituted that its tendency is to retain some more excellently than others. Thus the great classical scholar, Sir Richard Jebb, was unable to learn even the schoolboy mathematics required for the preliminary examination at Cambridge University, and a special act of the authorities was required in order to admit him.

7. The first method to be described has been detailed in Bhikku Ananda Metteya's "Training of the Mind" (EQUINOX, I. 5, pp. 28-59, and especially pp. 48-56). We have little to alter or to add.

Its most important result, as regards the Oath of the Abyss, is the freedom from all desire or clinging to everything which it gives. Its second result is to aid the adept in the second method, by supplying him with further data for his investigation.

8. The stimulation of memory useful in both practices is also achieved by simple meditation ("Liber E"), in a certain stage of which old memories arise unbidden. The adept may then practice this, stopping at that stage, and encouraging instead of suppressing the flashes of memory.

9. Zoroaster has said, "Explore the River of the Soul, whence or in what order you have come; so that although you have become a servant to the body, you may again rise to that Order (the A∴A∴) from which you descended, joining Works (Kamma) to Sacred Reason (the Tao)."

10. The Result of the Second Method is to show the Adept to what end his powers are destined. When he has passed the Abyss and become NEMO, the return of the current causes him "to appear in the Heaven of Jupiter as a morning star or as an evening star." In other words, he should discover what may be the nature of his work. Thus Mohammed was a Brother reflected in Netzach, Buddha a Brother reflected into Hod, or, as some say, Daath. The present manifestation of Frater P. to the outer is in Tiphareth, to the inner in the path of Leo.

11. First Method. Let the Exempt Adept first train himself to think backwards by external means, as set forth here following.

(a) Let him learn to write backwards, with either hand.

(b) Let him learn to walk backwards.

(c) Let him constantly watch, if convenient, cinematograph films, and listen to phonograph records, reversed, and let him so accustom himself to these that they appear natural, and appreciable as a whole.

(d) Let him practice speaking backwards; thus, for "I am He" let him say, "Eh ma I."

(e) Let him learn to read backwards. In this it is difficult to avoid cheating one's self, as an expert reader sees a sentence at a glance. Let his disciple read aloud to him backwards, slowly at first, then more quickly.

(f) Of his own ingenium let him devise other methods.

12. In this his brain will at first be overwhelmed by a sense of utter confusion; secondly, it will endeavour to avoid the difficulty by a trick. The brain will pretend to be working backwards when it is really normal. It is difficult to describe the nature of the trick, but it will be quite obvious to anyone who has done practices (a) or (b) for a day or two. They become quite easy, and he will think he is making progress, an illusion which close analysis will dispel.

13. Having begun to train his brain in this manner, and obtained some little success, let the Exempt Adept, seated in his Asana, think first of his present attitude, next of the act of being seated, next of his entering the room, next of his robing, et cetera, exactly as it happened. And let him most strenuously endeavour to think each act as happening backwards. It is not enough to think: "I am seated here, and before that I was standing, and before that I entered the room," etc. That series is the trick detected in the preliminary practices. The series must not run "ghi-def-abc," but "ihgfedcba": not "horse a is this" but "esroh a si siht." To obtain this thoroughly well, practice (c) is useful. The brain will be found to struggle constantly to right itself, soon accustoming itself to accept "esroh" as merely another glyph for "horse." This tendency must be constantly combatted.

14. In the early stages of this practice the endeavour should be to meticulous minuteness of detail in remembering actions; for the brain's habit of thinking forwards will at first be insuperable. Thinking of large and complex actions, then, will give a series which we may symbolically write "opqrstu-hijklmn-abcdefg." If these be split into detail, we shall have "stu-prq-o—mn-kl-hij—fg-cde-ab," which is much nearer to the ideal "utsrqponmlkjihgfedcba."

15. Capacities differ widely, but the Exempt Adept need have no reason to be discouraged if after a month's continuous labour he

find that now and again for a few seconds his brain really works backwards.

16. The Exempt Adept should concentrate his efforts upon obtaining a perfect picture of five minutes backwards rather than upon extending the time covered by his meditation. For this preliminary training of the brain is the Pons Asinorum of the whole process.

56

17. This five minutes' exercise being satisfactory, the Exempt Adept may extend the same at his discretion to cover an hour, a day, a week, and so on. Difficulties vanish before him as he advances; the extension from a day to the course of his whole life will not prove so difficult as the perfecting of the five minutes.

18. This practice should be repeated at least four times daily, and progress is shown firstly by the ever easier running of the brain, secondly by the added memories which arise.

19. It is useful to reflect during this practice, which in time becomes almost mechanical, upon the way in which effects spring from causes. This aids the mind to link its memories, and prepares the adept for the preliminary practice of the Second Method.

20. Having allowed the mind to return for some hundred times to the hour of birth, it should be encouraged to endeavour to penetrate beyond that period. If it be properly trained to run

backwards, there will be little difficulty in doing this, although it is one of the distinct steps in the practice.

21. It may be then that the memory will persuade the adept of some previous existence. Where this is possible, let it be checked by an appeal to facts, as follows.

22. It often occurs to men that on visiting a place to which they have never been, it appears familiar. This may arise from a confusion of thought or a slipping of the memory, but it is conceivably a fact.

If, then, the adept "remember" that he was in a previous life in some city, say Cracow, which he has in this life never visited, let him describe from memory the appearance of Cracow, and of its inhabitants, setting down their names. Let him further enter into the details of the city and its customs. And having done this with great minuteness, let him confirm the same by consultation with historians and geographers, or by a personal visit, remembering (both to the credit of his memory and its discredit) that historians, geographers, and himself are alike fallible. But let him not trust his memory to assert its conclusions as fact, and act thereupon, without most adequate confirmation.

23. This process of checking his memory should be practised with the earlier memories of childhood and youth by reference to the memories and records of others, always reflecting upon the

fallibility even of such safeguards.

24. All this being perfected, so that the memory reaches back into æons incalculably distant, let the Exempt Adept meditate upon the fruitlessness of all those years, and upon the fruit thereof, severing that which is transitory and worthless from that which is eternal. And it may be that he being but an Exempt Adept may hold all to be savourless and full of sorrow.

25. This being so, without reluctance will he swear the Oath of the Abyss.

26. Second Method. Let the Exempt Adept, fortified by the practice of the First Method, enter the preliminary practice of the Second Method.

27. Second Method. Preliminary Practices. Let him, seated in his Asana, consider any event, and trace it to its immediate causes. And let this be done very fully and minutely. Here, for example, is a body erect and motionless. Let the adept consider the many forces which maintain it; firstly, the attraction of the earth, of the sun, of the planets, of the farthest stars, nay, of every mote of dust in the room, one of which (could it be annihilated) would cause that body to move, although so imperceptibly. Also, the resistance of the floor, the pressure of the air, and all other external conditions. Secondly, the internal forces which sustain it, the vast and complex machinery of the skeleton, the muscles, the

blood, the lymph, the marrow, all that makes up a man. Thirdly, the moral and intellectual forces involved, the mind, the will, the consciousness. Let him continue this with unremitting ardour, searching Nature, leaving nothing out.

28. Next let him take one of the immediate causes of his position, and trace out its equilibrium. For example, the will. What determines the will to aid in holding the body erect and motionless?

29. This being determined, let him choose one of the forces which determined his will, and trace out that in similar fashion; and let this process be continued for many days until the interdependence of all things is a truth assimilated in his inmost being.

30. This being accomplished, let him trace out his own history with special reference to the causes of each event. And in this practice he may neglect to some extent the universal forces which at all times act on all, as for example the attraction of masses, and let him concentrate his attention upon the principal and determining or effective causes.

For instance, he is seated, perhaps, in a country place in Spain. Why? Because Spain is warm and suitable for meditation, and because cities are noisy and crowded. Why is Spain warm? and why does he wish to meditate? Why choose warm Spain rather than warm India? To the last question: Because Spain is nearer to his home. Then why is his home near Spain? Because his parents were Germans. And why did they go to Germany? And so during the whole meditation.

31. On another day, let him begin with a question of another kind, and every day devise new questions, not only concerning his present situation, but also abstract questions. Thus let him connect the prevalence of water upon the surface of the globe with its necessity to such life as we know, with the specific gravity and other physical properties of water, and let him perceive ultimately through all this the necessity and concord of things, not concord as the schoolmen of old believed, making all things for man's benefit or convenience, but the essential mechanical concord whose final law is inertia. And in these meditations let him avoid as if it were the plague any speculation sentimental or fantastic.

32. Second Method. The Practice Proper. Having then perfected in his mind these conceptions, let him apply them to his own career, forging the links of memory into the chain of necessity.

And let this be his final question: To what purpose am I fitted? Of what service can my being prove to the Brothers of the A∴A∴ if I cross the Abyss, and am admitted to the City of the Pyramids?

33. Now that he may clearly understand the nature of this

question, and the method of solution, let him study the reasoning of the anatomist who reconstructs an animal from a single bone. To take a simple example.

34. Suppose, having lived all my life among savages, a ship is cast upon the shore and wrecked. Undamaged among the cargo is a "Victoria." What is its use? The wheels speak of roads, their slimness of smooth roads, the brake of hilly roads. The shafts show that it was meant to be drawn by an animal, their height and length suggest an animal of the size of a horse. That the carriage is open suggests a climate tolerable at any rate for part of the year. The height of the box suggests crowded streets, or the spirited character of the animal employed to draw it. The cushions indicate its use to convey men rather than merchandise; its hood that rain sometimes falls, or that the sun is at times powerful. The springs would imply considerable skill in metals; the varnish much attainment in that craft.

35. Similarly, let the adept consider of his own case. Now that he is on the point of plunging into the Abyss, a giant Why? confronts him with uplifted club.

36. There is no minutest atom of his composition which can be withdrawn from him without making him some other than what he is, no useless moment in his past. Then what is his future? The "Victoria" is not a waggon; it is not intended for carting hay. It is

not a sulky; it is useless in trotting races.

37. So the adept has military genius, or much knowledge of Greek: how do these attainments help his purpose, or the purpose of the Brothers? He was put to death by Calvin, or stoned by Hezekiah; as a snake he was killed by a villager, or as an elephant slain in battle under Hamilcar. How do such memories help him? Until he have thoroughly mastered the reason for every incident in his past, and found a purpose for every item of his present equipment, he cannot truly answer even those Three Questions that were first put to him, even the Three Questions of the Ritual of the Pyramid; he is not ready to swear the Oath of the Abyss.

38. But being thus enlightened, let him swear the Oath of the Abyss; yea, let him swear the Oath of the Abyss.

LIBER III
VEL
JVGORVM

A∴A∴

O

0. Behold the Yoke upon the neck of the Oxen! Is it not thereby that the Field shall be ploughed? The Yoke is heavy but joineth together them that are separate—Glory to Nuit and to Hadit, and to Him that hath given us the Symbol of the Rosy Cross! Glory unto the Lord of the Word Abrahadabra, and Glory unto Him that hath given us the Symbol of the Ankh, and of the Cross within the Circle!

1. These are the Beasts wherewith thou must plough the Field; the Unicorn, the Horse, and the Ox. And these shalt thou yoke in a triple yoke that is governed by One Whip.

2. Now these Beasts run wildly upon the earth and are not easily obedient to the Man.

3. Nothing shall be said here of Cerberus, the great Beast of Hell that is every one of these and all of these, even as Athanasius hath foreshadowed. For this matter is not of Tiphereth without, but Tiphereth within.

(I.e. the matter of Cerberus).

I

0. The Unicorn is speech. Man, rule thy Speech! How else shalt thou master the Son, and answer the Magician at the Right Hand

Gateway of the Crown?

1. Here are practices. Each may last for a week or more.

α. Avoid using some common word, such as "and" or "the" or "but"; use a paraphrase.

β. Avoid using some letter of the alphabet, such as "t" or "s" or "m"; use a paraphrase.

γ. Avoid using the pronouns and adjectives of the first person; use a paraphrase.

Of thine own ingenium devise others.

2. On each occasion that thou art betrayed into saying that thou art sworn to avoid, cut thyself sharply upon the wrist or forearm with a razor; even as thou shouldst beat a disobedient dog. Feareth not the Unicorn the claws and tooth of the Lion?

> *This practice must not be dodged; e.g. (1) by failing to cut at the first moment of discovery, and giving oneself (so to say) "I'll make 10 cuts when I've made 10 slips," or (2) by "I'll make a slip in view of the immediate need: I don't mind the pain of a cut." The object of the whole exercise is to create a sentinel to stand watch at the threshold of the Mind: with this in view one should be able to study the psychology of the practice in detail and arrange matters so as to obtain the best result possible.*

3. Thine arm then serveth thee both for a warning and for a record. Thou shalt write down thy daily progress in these

practices, until thou art perfectly vigilant at all times over the least word that slippeth from thy tongue.

Thus bind thyself, and thou shalt be for ever free.

II

0. The Horse is Action. Man, rule thou thine Action. How else shalt thou master the Father and answer the Fool at the Left Hand Gateway of the Crown?

1. Here are practices. Each may last for a week or more.

α. Avoid lifting the left arm above the waist.

β. Avoid crossing the legs.

Of thine own ingenium devise others.

2. On each occasion that thou art betrayed into doing that thou art sworn to avoid, cut thyself sharply upon the wrist or forearm with a razor; even as thou shouldst beat a disobedient dog. Feareth not the Horse the claws and tooth of the Camel?

3. Thine arm then serveth thee both for a warning and for a record. Thou shalt write down thy daily progress in these practices, until thou art perfectly vigilant at all times over the least action that slippeth from thy fingers.

Thus bind thyself, and thou shalt be for ever free.

III

0. The Ox is Thought. Man, rule thou thy Thought! How else

shalt thou master the Holy Spirit, and answer the High Priestess in the Middle Gateway of the Crown?

1. Here are practices. Each may last for a week or more.

α. Avoid thinking of a definite subject and all things connected with it, and let that subject be one which commonly occupies much of thy thought, being frequently stimulated by sense-perceptions or the conversation of others.

β. By some device, such as the changing of thy ring from one finger to another, create in thyself two personalities, the thoughts of one being within entirely different limits from that of the other, the common ground being the necessities of life.

For instance, let A be a man of strong passions, skilled in the Holy Qabalah, a vegetarian, and a keen 'reactionary' politician; let B be a bloodless and ascetic thinker, occupied with business and family cares, an eater of meat, and a keen progressive politician. Let no thought proper to 'A' arise when the ring is on the 'B' finger; and vice versa.

Of thine own ingenium devise others.

2. On each occasion that thou art betrayed into thinking that thou art sworn to avoid, cut thyself sharply upon the wrist or forearm with a razor; even as thou shouldst beat a disobedient dog. Feareth not the Ox the Goad of the Ploughman?

3. Thine arm then serveth thee both for a warning and for a record. Thou shalt write down thy daily progress in these practices, until thou art perfectly vigilant at all times over the least thought that ariseth in thy brain.

Thus bind thyself, and thou shalt be for ever free.

ARATVM SECVRVM

(Fra —— after one week avoiding the first person. His fidelity is good; his vigilance bad. Not nearly good enough to pass).

[Lat., "careless plough" or "secure plough."]

P.S. An XV ☉ in c An excellent practice is to control the means of expression.

Thus, challenge the world to make you smile.

LIBER
XXXVI
THE
STAR
SAPPHIRE

A∴A∴

Let the Adept be armed with his Magick Rood [and provided with his Mystic Rose].

In the centre, let him give the L.V.X. signs; or if he know them, if he will and dare do them, and can keep silent about them, the signs of N.O.X. being the signs of Puer, Vir, Puella, Mulier. Omit the sign I.R.

Then let him advance to the East, and make the Holy Hexagram,

> saying: PATER ET MATER UNUS DEUS ARARITA.

Let him go round to the South, make the Holy Hexagram, and

> say: MATER ET FILIUS UNUS DEUS ARARITA.

Let him go round to the West, make the Holy Hexagram, and

> say: FILIUS ET FILIA UNUS DEUS ARARITA.

67

Let him go round to the North, make the Holy Hexagram, and

> then say: FILIA ET PATER UNUS DEUS ARARITA.

Let him return to the Centre, and so to The Centre of All [making the Rosy Cross as he may know how] saying:

ARARITA ARARITA ARARITA.

[In this the Signs shall be those of Set Triumphant and of Baphomet. Also shall Set appear in the Circle. Let him drink of the Sacrament and let him communicate the same.]

Then let him say:

OMNIA IN DUOS: DUO IN UNUM: UNUS IN NIHIL: HÆC NEC QUATUOR NEC OMNIA NEC DUO NEC UNUS NEC NIHIL SUNT.

GLORIA PATRI ET MATRI ET FILIO ET FILIÆ ET SPIRITUI SANCTO EXTERNO ET SPIRITUI SANCTO INTERNO UT ERAT EST ERIT IN SÆCULA SÆCULORUM SEX IN UNO PER NOMEN SEPTEM IN UNO ARARITA.

Let him then repeat the signs of L.V.X. but not the signs of N.O.X.: for it is not he that shall arise in the Sign of Isis Rejoicing.

* * * * *

The Star Sapphire corresponds with the Star-Ruby of Chapter 25, 36 being the square of 6, as 25 is of 5. This chapter gives the real and perfect Ritual of the Hexagram. It would be improper to comment further upon an official ritual of the A∴A∴.

Appendix A: Zelator Tasks and Oath

The task of the Zelator is to consolidate control of posture and breath, deepen meditation practice, and begin practical magical work on one's own responsibility.

The official task as set forth in Liber CLXXXV includes the following key elements: The Zelator must pass examinations in asana and pranayama demonstrating specific attainments beyond the Neophyte standard. The minimum duration of the grade is eight months, and advancement occurs by authority of the Order when the task is satisfactorily completed. The Zelator must acquire proficiency in the practices of Liber HHH and related meditations. The construction of the magical dagger is assigned to this grade, marking the beginning of self-directed practical work.

The Oath of the Zelator, in its essential structure, commits the aspirant to continue the Great Work at the level of the foundations of one's own being. The Zelator pledges service to Neophytes and self-denial on their behalf, recognizing that teaching is itself a form of learning. The long-term aspiration expressed in the oath is toward the knowledge and conversation of the Holy Guardian Angel.

The full wording of the Zelator task and oath appears in Liber

CLXXXV, printed in the Probationer volume of this series.

Appendix B: Notes on Asana and Pranayama beyond Neophyte

The Neophyte was expected to achieve basic competence in asana and pranayama as outlined in Liber E. This meant establishing a stable posture that could be held without excessive discomfort, learning simple timed breathing, and developing elementary awareness of the body and its energies. The standard was functional: the Neophyte needed to be able to sit still long enough to perform basic concentration exercises without the body constantly intruding on attention.

At Zelator, the standards increase significantly. The posture must now be held with greater precision and for longer periods.

Fidgeting, pain-driven adjustments, and restlessness should be largely overcome. The breathing cycles become longer and more structured, and the Zelator begins to integrate breath with concentration rather than treating them as entirely separate disciplines. Where the Neophyte learned to breathe with attention, the Zelator learns to use breath as a tool for directing mental and vital force.

Liber RV introduces practices that go beyond the foundational work of Liber E. The breathing ratios become more complex, moving from simple equal counts to proportional cycles. The text introduces the integration of breath with mantra and visualization, and develops the concept of circulating force through the body.

Liber RV should be understood as building upon Liber E, not replacing it.

Practical guidance for the Zelator's breath work: Increase the length of your breathing cycles gradually, allowing the body to adapt rather than forcing progress. Never strain to the point of panic, muscular collapse, or loss of control. Keep detailed records of each practice session, noting posture, time of day, breathing ratio, and any physical or mental effects observed. Watch for common warning signs such as persistent headaches, unusual agitation, or disrupted sleep; if these occur, reduce the intensity of practice.

The work done at Zelator prepares the body and breath for the more demanding practices of Practicus and Philosophus. The Qabalah work and devotional practices of those grades require a foundation of physical stability and energetic control. A Zelator who has not genuinely mastered asana and pranayama will find the later work increasingly difficult. Build the foundation now; it will bear the weight of everything that follows.

Appendix C: Recommended Additional

Reading

Raja Yoga by Swami Vivekananda. A systematic and accessible treatment of concentration and meditation that helps contextualize the asana and pranayama work in a broader yogic framework.

The Shiva Samhita. Traditional hatha yoga manual that illuminates the physical and energetic dimensions of practice. Read for orientation rather than as instructions to follow immediately.

The Spiritual Guide by Miguel de Molinos. A classic Western text on interior practice and contemplative silence. The approach to quieting the mind parallels aspects of the meditation work assigned at this grade.

The Tao Te Ching. The foundational text of Taoism, relevant here because Liber XXVII draws upon the symbolism of the Tao.

The Book of Lies by Aleister Crowley. A collection of short chapters, many of which illuminate concepts relevant to Zelator work. The cryptic style requires meditation rather than casual reading.

Eight Lectures on Yoga by Aleister Crowley. A more accessible introduction to yoga from the Thelemic perspective, useful for understanding how the physical practices relate to the broader magical work.

These readings are supplementary, not required. The core work of the grade is in the Libri themselves and in consistent practice. Reading should support practice, not substitute for it.

COLOPHON

Compiled by

Frater Lachesis Peyton

"Do what thou wilt shall be the whole of the Law. Love is the law, love under will."